THEOCHARIS M. PROVATAKIS

METEORA

HISTORY OF THE MONASTERIES AND MONASTICISM

MICHALIS TOUBIS EDITIONS - ATHENS

© Copyright   MICHALIS TOUBIS PUBLICATIONS S.A.
Nisiza Karela, Koropi, Attiki, Telephone: +30 210 6029974,
Fax: +30 210 6646856, Web Site: http://www.toubis.gr

ISBN: 960-540-095-2

Here on those barren rocks, which became palaces for thousands of ascetics, Orthodox monks have learnt to be wise in thought and humble in will

CONTENTS

INTRODUCTION

Heteora has not only been, ever since the 11th century, a place of prayer where obedience is practised, the will is disciplined and faith is forged, but it has acted as a magnet to attract thousands of visitors from all over the world to the 'stone forest' which it has to show. The strangeness and grandeur of this place, the security and peace which is experienced by everyone who settles there and the desire of many to forsake the world and retire to places of quietness created the monasteries of Meteora, which, with the passing of time, became a powerful magnet and spiritual oasis, where many travellers on the road of life have found spiritual refreshment and inner peace. Even today the rocks of Meteora are no less than spiritual training grounds and arenas where faith is fashioned, sin is driven out and the personality is forged.

A considerable number of studies of the Meteora complex have already been written. In these, various researchers have tried in their own way to present the historic religious houses of this 'stone forest' as they have seen them and as they have experienced Orthodox monasticism.

The work which follows is brief, and it ventures to give authoritative information to each visitor on where he should go and what he should see in the region of Meteora. Consequently its exclusive aim is to inform the visitor in a brief, but clear and complete, manner of the history, archaeology, art, tradition and physical beauties of a spot where the first and greatest doctor of antiquity, Asclepius, was born, where classical civilization developed, where Byzantium was honoured, where Orthodox monasticism took its final form, and where, finally, it played an honourable role in the uprising of 1821. Thus this work is not so much an exclusively scholarly monograph, as a popularized illustrated guide based on scholarship. A particular effort has been made to give an account of Orthodox monasticism from the time when it made its appearance on the beautiful soil of Thessaly, and particularly on the rocks of Meteora and the surrounding area, down to the present day.

Theocharis M. Provatakis

THE METEORA COMPLEX

Topography

An ideal spot for spiritual exercise and meditation, Meteora is nothing other than a group of lofty and precipitous rocks crowned with monasteries, retreats and cells, while its various caves have been turned into hermits' cells for Orthodox monasticism since the 11th century. It is situated near Kalambaka at the point where the Peneus river flows out into the beautiful plain of Thessaly and at a height of some 300 metres from the valley. The landscape is delightful and overwhelming — perhaps one of the most beautiful on earth. As a natural phenomenon, however, it is unique. A thousand or so vertiginous rocks, which from a distance look like a forest of stone, spring up unexpectedly before one, producing a feeling of 'trembling and astonishment' and leading one to deep reflection. This formation, and more generally the creation of the plain of Trikala is, according to experts, to be ascribed to the so-called tritogenic period which is lost in the mists of 60,000 years ago. The water which formed a closed lake forced itself out through the opening of Tempe, whence it flowed into the Aegean, thus creating the features of the area, which only came to be inhabited much later.

History

Thessaly has been recognized as the site of the most ancient habitation in Greece, while Trikki can be traced back to the very earliest period. It is mentioned in Homer as having taken part in the Trojan War, while other historians and geographers (Strabo, Herodotus, Livy etc.) give specific information about the area. It was here that in classical times lived the famous doctor of antiquity Asclepius. Here with his sons Machaon and Podalirus he founded the Asclepeion and they treated their patients. During the Hellenistic period the area played an important role in the life and development of Greece. Fine mosaics, coins, inscriptions, vessels, sarcophagi and small works of art, together with other objects, dating from the Roman period have been found.

During the Byzantine period the area, and particularly Meteora, contributed substantially to the building up of a strong monastic centre. The monastic life —that is, retirement from the human community and voluntary confinement to desert places— is traceable in Christianity to the earliest centuries. It has not been established when exactly monasticism made its first appearance at Meteora. However, we know that in the 11th century there were monks and hermitages in the area. The monks lived in caves or in small cells, and every Sunday ('Kyriaki' in Greek) and major feastday descended to celebrate the Liturgy together at Doubiani, which was thus named 'Kyriako'. Somewhat later, as the number of monks increased, the Retreat of Stagi was established. The name Stagi is derived either from 'sitagogos' ('wheat transporter'), since the Thessalian plain was rich in wheat, or from a corruption of the words 'stous aghious' ('the place of the saints'), 'st'aghious' becoming 'stagous'. From the 12th century began the systematic organization of the Retreat, which was under the jurisdiction of the bishopric of Stagi.

In the 14th century Serbian princes, who were at that time the lords of Thessaly, accorded many privileges to the Retreat and it was ruled by a Trotos (Prior) who, at that period, lived in the monastery at Doubiani.

It was at this time that an important figure, a monk from Mt. Athos called Athanasios, arrived at Meteora, and founded the first monastery on the rock known as Platylithos. On this impressive rock, which rises 613 metres above sea level and 413 metres above Kalambaka and which dominates the whole landscape, Athanasios built his monastery. He called the rock 'Meteora' ('in the air') because it seemed to hang suspended between earth and heaven; hence it is that even today the whole complex of rocks is known as 'Meteora'.

Thus, Athanasios, having built a chapel and a few cells, gathered together 14 monks from the surrounding rocks, organized a brother-

The Thessalian plain. Engraving of 1846.

hood and laid the first foundations of a common monastic life. A little later the successor of the Serbian prince Stephen Dusan, who had granted a number of privileges to Meteora, was Symeon Ouresis, who followed the same policy. When, later, his son John Ouresis became a monk and settled at Meteora under the name of Joasaph, the situation changed. Joasaph was a friend of Athanasios and the two of them brought the monastery to a highly flourishing state. The church was decorated with fine murals and the monastery equipped with towers, an infirmary, cells, water-tanks and other buildings. The number of monks began to increase, and later, with the community constantly growing, they also had to enlarge the central church, which they called the 'Katholikon'. The new church was on a large scale and used the older one as its sanctuary. After the death of Athanasios and Joasaph, the Orthodox Church, as a result of the miracles which they had performed and the holy lives which they had led, canonized them as saints. Thus Meteora had become a centre of monasticism and Orthodox religious life in the beautiful plain of Thessaly.

At the same period, another monk, Varlaam, conceived the idea of building another large monastery on the tall rock opposite. This was completed some 200 years later by the brothers Nectarios and Theophanis of Ioannina.

During the centuries which followed monasticism at Meteora grew, with the result that a large number of other monasteries were built. In 1490 the position of Protos of the Retreat was abolished and all the retreats, monasteries, cells and hermitages were brought under the authority of the Monastery of the Transfiguration, the most important.

The 17th century unfortunately saw the beginning of the decline of monasticism at Meteora which resulted in the diminution of the number of monasteries and of monks.

Today six (6) monasteries continue to function and can be visited by pilgrims — who must be soberly dressed. These are: The Transfiguration, St. Varlaam, Holy Trinity, St. Stephen the Protomartyr, St. Nicholas Anapafsas and Rousanou.

Apart from the above monasteries which continue in use today, there are ruins of other monasteries where scores of monks lived in former times. Uninhabited today and more or less in ruins are the following monasteries of Meteora:

1.The Monastery of St. George Mandilas. 2.The Monastery of St. Nicholas Bandovas or Kophinas. 3.The Monastery of the Holy Spirit. 4.The Monastery of the Presentation of Christ. 5.The Monastery of Paliopanayia. 6.The Retreat of Doubiani. 7.The Monastery of the Holy Apostles. 8. The Monastery of St. Gregory. 9. The Monastery of St. Antony. 10. The Monastery of the Almighty. 11.The Monastery of St. John the Baptist. 12. The Monastery of the Highest in the Heavens or the Calligraphers. 13. The Monastery of St. Modestos. 14. The Monastery of St. Peter's Chains, and 16. The Monastery of St. Demetrius.

GOING TO METEORA

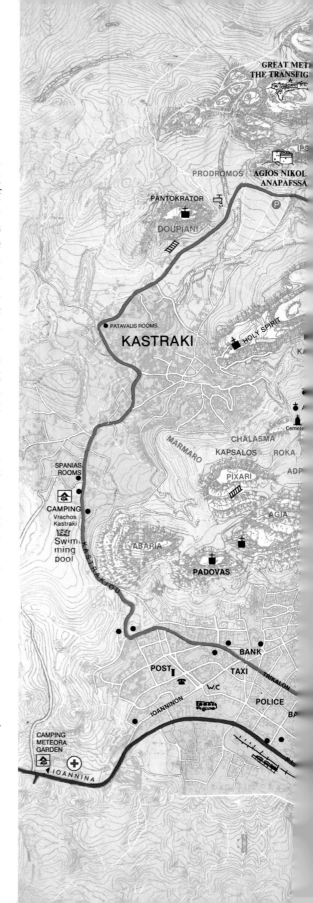

Leaving behind picturesque Kastraki, one follows an uphill road in order to reach the summits of the rocks above, where the monasteries are situated. The road is like a huge snake which winds among the ravines, hauls itself over the very few cultivated hills, glides round precipitous yellow-green rocks and arrives at Meteora. As you go up on foot or in a car, you find that the hills give off scents at all seasons of the year. All around everything is calm and peaceful, while a light wind accompanies one's thoughts. Right and left wild and towering rocks make their presence felt. Ancient, half-collapsed wooden ladders stick out from the very few clefts in these multi-coloured rocks, testifying to the presence of ascetics there in former times. It is said that in one of the caves, which can be seen in a rock on the right as you go up with wooden ladders hanging down, the ascetic monks used to stay for months on end without coming down at all, thus punishing their bodies for some act of disobedience or for allowing their thoughts to take flight back to the world.

The magic of the journey from Kastraki to the monasteries is sheer enjoyment. It takes about two hours and transports you into a land of dreams. The greenery of every shade terminates in idyllic lines with sheer rocks and red formations springing from it. The beauty of nature which one is enjoying is a blend of gentle southern and wild northern lines, which produce a feeling of ecstasy of the spirit.

▬▬▬	Central road
▬▬▬	Asphalt road
═══	Road
- - - -	Path
☗	Church
🏛	Monastery
◼	Monastery (ruins)
⌂	Campsite
🚌	Bus station
Ⓟ	Car park
🚃	Railway
✚	Hospital
🚰	Spring
▨	Steps
⛪	Cemetery
●	Hotel
▮	Post Office
	Telephone
▦	Icon shop

VARLAÁM
595

DRAKOSPILIA

KELARAKIA

PLAKES

W.C

TERA

PALEOKRANIES

ROUSSANOU

KOUMARIES

PSAROPETRA
PANORAMA

SFICA

KASTANES

ASSES
KIA

AGIA TRIAS

GIN
KOLAOS

MODI

620

ALISSOS

AGIA TRIAS
570

AGIA TRIAS

URLOTI

SOPOTOS

CHURCH OF THE
DORMITION OF THE VIRGIN

AGIOS STEFANOS
575

POULIANA

MANDRIA

LABAKA

TRIKALON

ICONS SHOP

ABELIA

MIRA

CAMPING
KALAMBAKA

METEORA

INTERNATIONAL
CAMPING RIZOS
1 KM

ICONS WORKSHOP

TRIKALA

The Monasteries.

After this enchanting approach, you arrive at some lonely heights from which can be seen a veritable forest of huge rocks crowned with monasteries which are in mysterious harmony with the landscape. The monks are always ready to receive you in the parlour, offering you the hospitality which the example of Abraham and Greek tradition demand. Up there solitude and silence are the rule. Wherever you look you will be aware of an unparalleled peace and calmness, exactly as happens with a star-filled sky in autumn which is filled with voiceless ecstasy. There on those barren and inhospitable rocks, which became palaces for thousands of ascetic Orthodox monks have learnt to be wise in thought and humble in will. Within them lives another world, free from the violence of the elements and unbounded by time, from which each monk can draw power to resist the elements of nature and hymn the creation through the cataclysm in which he is often in danger of being lost himself.

St. Nicholas Anapafsas. Engraving dated 1846.

The Churches.

s soon as you find yourself in the dark churches of the Monasteries of Meteora, you are seized by a feeling which is a mixture of faith and reverence. The holiness of the place, with its carved wooden and gilded screens, its marvellous icons, the cycle of the life of Christ, above, its wealth of murals drawn from the dogmatic, historical and liturgical cycle of the Orthodox Church, creates an atmosphere of profound faith in the Creator. Everything there is characterized by extreme cleanliness and reverence. The ascetic forms which are portrayed on the screens and on the walls seem to speak to you in the play of the flickering light of the candles and that little which comes from the lamps. An atmosphere of the divine rules everywhere. Involutarily you whisper words of prayer, directing your thoughts to the Creator. You have the feeling of talking with Him; you have left the earth and your thoughts are in the heavens. The dim light which comes from the sky-lights in the domes and from the few windows is the mysterious link between heaven and earth. It is here that you believe that you are in heavenly places and experience the mystical forces which work in the soul, with the result that the barriers which separate the human spirit and nature are broken down. Your soul is possessed by awe and love as an expression of the experience of the unapproachable. You are aware of an internal light and a peace-giving joy which are difficult to describe. God is close to you, He is within you and you are in mystical communication with Him. It is at this moment that you find yourself.

The Sacristies.

fter the churches of the monasteries of Meteora the monks will take you to see the sacristies and the libraries. Hung on the walls or displayed in show-cases you will find miniature works of art and painting which have taken great patience and persistance to complete to admire. Parchment gospels and large numbers of manuscripts of a historical and liturgical nature, portable icons, the products of skilful hands and a powerful imagination, Good Friday bier cloths, vestments embroidered in gold with an abundance of grace and dexterity, valuable silver and fire-gilded cases, a variety of fine crosses in gold, enamel or silver with precious stones and pearls, and hundreds of other liturgical and ecclesiastical objects are preserved and shown with reverence to every pilgrim.

Wooden gold-inlaid cross.

The Libraries.

n the libraries the monks preserve valuable manuscripts and hundreds of documents. The majority of handwritten codices, which are of parchment, deal with various religious, historical, medical, philosophical and mathematical matters.

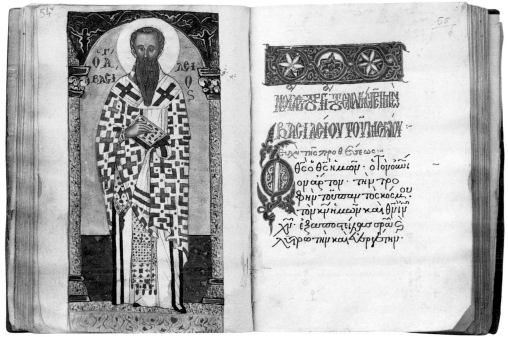

Manuscript Gospel from the Great Meteoron Monastery (17th century).

There are, of course, also those which are written on paper, dating from the 14th century. Some of these codices contain remarkable miniatures preserved in excellent condition. There are also gold bulls, decrees of the Patriarch of Constantinople, lead bulls, patriarchal decrees etc., which testify to the generous benefactions of emperors and patriarchs over the centuries.

Thus the indomitable will of the monks to preserve and pass on what they had received from their predecessors, their foresight and cunning in difficult times and above all their self-sacrifice have saved these relics, which constitute an incaluable national ancestral treasure.

During the most recent study carried out in the monasteries of Meteora 1124 codices were recorded and classified by N. Veis, distributed among the monasteries as follows: Monastery of the Great Meteora 610, Monastery of Varlam 269, Monastery of St. Stephen 103, Monastery of the Holy Trinity 47, Monastery of Rousanou 52, and Monastery of St. Nicholas Anapafsas 43.

From the Passion of Christ (14th century).

19

The View from the Terraces of Meteora.

hen you are on the peaks of the gigantic, dark rocks which are the sites of the terraces of the monasteries of Meteora and as your eye takes in the peaceful plain of Thessaly, your heart beats with an altered pace. It seems as though these vast rock formations which rear up around you are ready for some mighty battle in which their every movement will create some cosmic upheaval in the Thessalian plain, which reclines below in all its greenery as though nothing at all were happening.

The ravishing spectacle of the rocks with their green carpet around them produces feelings of wonder mixed with awe, precisely because from up there man feels his helplessness before the wonders of the Creator. At the same time one has a sense of the sublime and the beautiful. The beautiful can be expressed in measurable terms — its content and form are in complete harmony. Its beauty is static. As the Parthenon is in art, so in nature the quiet plain of Thessaly lies before one in the embrace of the Peneus river.

The element of the sublime comes from the sight of those lofty rocks on whose summit you are and where you feel that you are between earth and heaven. As you look down at the green plain, you are aware of an ideal balance, while an Olympian calm takes hold of you at the sight of this wonderful creation. As you gaze at the gigantic rocks which rise around you, you experience a state of spiritual elevation and reflection.

At the same time, the sense of the sublime creates in each monk and in each visitor a great tenseness of the emotions which seek to find some outlet. This outlet comes after strong feelings which have spiritual implications for the mystical life and the peace of Meteora. Thus the beauty of the plain addresses itself to the perception and the intellect, while the sublime speaks to the emotions and the soul, in order to be better understood.

On the Balconies of St. Stephen's and the Great Meteoro.

he view from the monasteries of St. Stephen and the Great Meteoro is indescribable. If you pause there a while to look below you, you will experience an inner peace and be led to higher spheres. The view which you will have is hard to conceive in its extent and unparalleled in grandeur. It is perhaps the best compensation for the difficulty of the ascent. Picturesque Kastraki lies 'at your feet', historic Kalambaka is 'in front of you' and the green and peaceful plain of Thessaly virtually surrounds you.

A little further off the River Peneus, which for so many centuries has played along its charming course, creates a phenomenon unique in beauty and delight.

Everything up there evinces a certain grandeur and, taken all together, produces an imposing harmony.

The greenness of the plain in its abundance is restful, the quiet is purifying, the impressiveness of the place is overwhelming, its sanctity is a blessing and all together these lift you above material things and bring you close to the Creator.

Your soul, broken down by contradictions and uncertainties and wearied by the constant attempt to satisfy what is unfulfilled, longs for the unknown, the feelings for which create a saving counterbalance.

The View of the Heavens.

f you then turn your gaze to the heavens, you will be overtaken by a different sensation — a sensation made more intense by the celestial limit of the horizon which houses the mute and lofty dome of the heavens. Your own soul begins to rise to that heavenly dome and accommodate itself to the boundlessness of that silent plain, while a variety of emotions crowd in upon the heart. Through this antithesis of emotions of awe and wonder a feeling of ecstasy springs up and this is converted into 'fear and astonishment' if a storm should suddenly break. The sky immediately darkens and the rain begins to pour down ceaselessly.

The wind begins to whistle around you and begins to beat relentlessly on the vast rocks scoured by the rain, while lightning like snakes furrows the horizon. The torrential rain and the strong wind on the one hand and the mass of the rocks which surround you on the other create within you a mystical symphony and lead you involuntarily to the awakakening of your subconscious, under the rule of the silence.

This interior silence, though you try to stifle its voice in the noise of the rain, the wind and the thunder, begins to speak to you in a thousand different ways. Then you notice that the water which rages against the rocks produces small cararacts which roar down among the rocks and their outcrops with a primeval clamour.

The floods which lash all around form dangerous rivulets and create small torrents which find their way into the Peneus.

At that moment you feel exaltation, under the influence of the symphony created by the combination of rain, thunder and wind. You shudder to the depths of your being when the thunder jolts the green and ashen-coloured rocks and the lightning suddenly illuminates them to their base.

You feel a spiritual upheaval when you participate in these commotions of the heavens which the Creator directs.

It is then that you feel loss, because certainly you cannot oppose yourself to the battle of the elements, nor can you take it in with your mind. You feel the need to be down in the plain to participate aesthetically in the action of the elements, as when you listen to the dramatic climax of a musical symphony. Then, safe from the elements of nature and without the trumpet-calls of terror and the fear of the lightning, you experience a spiritual force of superiority rising up within you which mounts freely on high, full of joy and drunk with ecstasy.

Koziakas and Meteora.

In the distance, facing the monasteries of Meteora, Koziakas, the subject of many songs, rises. Its great, sharp rocks and innumerable peaks are sometimes struggling to pierce the clouds and at others to lance the bright blue Greek sky. The sparkling white villages at the foot of Koziakas and in the places sheltered from the North winds on the plain complete the beauty of the land of Thessaly.

As you look at all this and see around you a whole forest of green and ash-coloured masses, on the peaks of which are monasteries with roofs and caves, wooden galleries suspended in the air and balconies which crouch on the edge of the abyss, you do not known what to marvel at first. You are surprised by their vastness and absorbed by their grandeur, allowing yourself experiences which are unrepeatable.

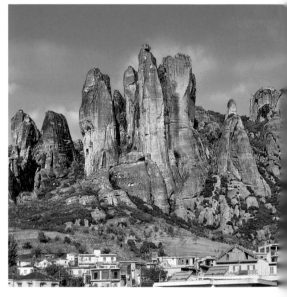

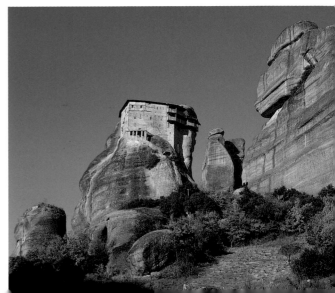

THE ORGANIZATION OF MONASTICISM AT METEORA

The name Meteora is not met with in ancient times. It was used for the first time by the proprietor of the Monastery of the Transfiguration, Blessed Athanasios of Meteora, who in 1344 called the 'Platys Lithos' (the Broad Rock) 'Meteora'. This name prevailed a little later and signified the rock or rocks, accordingly, of the present-day Meteora.

When exactly Meteora was first in habited by monks is not known. The historical documents and other evidence which exists portray monasticism organized in retreats from the ninth century.

The monks, having set up initially small places for prayer —called 'prosefchadia'— went every Sunday to the 'Kyriako', that is, a common church, to celebrate the Divine Liturgy. Thus ascetic monasticism came to be established at Meteora. Other information names as the first ascetic here a certain Varnavas, who between 950 and 965 founded the Retreat of the Holy Spirit. A little later, round about 1020 A.D., tradition tradition goes, the monk Andronikos from Crete built a hermitage on the rock occupied today by the Transfiguration monastery, while other monks established the Retreat of Stagi, which they called Doubiani, around 1160. Some two hundred years later the monk Varlaam founded the Monastery of the Three Hierarchs and the Monastery of All Saints, while at the same period other monks established other religious houses and lived in them.

With the passage of time the monastic community grew, the number of monasteries increased to 24 and they received support from various benefactions and privileges accorded to them by lords, princes and patriarchs at various periods. The 17th century saw monasticism at its most flourishing at Meteora, but today there are six monasteries in operation and here the few remaining monks fight for their survival and renewal.

The Aim of the Monks

The visiting pilgrim, by staying a little while with the monks and talking with them, discovers great truths. The prayers, the fasts, the vigils, the acts of charity and the other Christian virtues do not, by themselves, represent the aim of the Orthodox Christian life. These are only necessary means, as one monk Meteora told us, since they are performed in the name of Christ for the success of this aim. The true aim of the Orthodox Christian life is the acquisition of the Holy Spirit. The monk does nothing other than this. He lives in a constant efort to draw closer to God. St. John Climacus (7th century) says epigramatically 'a monk is a constant violation of nature and a guard upon the senses'. If, the monk continued to explain, the heart of the monk is to be 'fervent', the conscious mind must remain apathetic, since the mind keeps watch on the heart. Consequently, the heart, in accordance with Orthodox teaching, is the centre of human life and the source of the active powers both in the intellect and the will. It is the point from which the whole of the spiritual life springs and to which it tends. The heart, according to Macarius of Egypt, is 'the workshop of good and evil'. It is a vessel which contains every kind of wrong, but at the same time it can be said of it that 'there is God, there are the angels, there is life and kingship, there is light and the postles, there is the treasury of grace'.

The Penitence of the Monks

enitence for the monk is not a passing moment or a temporary state, but is a perpetual condition, as a monk of Meteora explained to us. It is a second birth which God gives after baptism, a way of return to the Father. The more the monk is united with God, the more aware he is of his own ignorance, the more he is perfected and knows his own imperfection. The result of repentance is internal contrition and tears. It is at the same time the beginning of eternal life. Tears purify nature, since repentance is not only our effort in our pain, but the illuminating gift of the Holy Spirit who penetrates and transforms our heart. The prayer of the monk is the motive force in all his efforts in the spiritual life. Thus union with God can only be achieved through prayer, since prayer is the personal relationship of man with God, and through it man meets personally with him, according to Isaac the Syrian. There it is that man becomes acquainted with Him and loves Him. Knowledge and love are closely related in Orthodox monasticism.

The Prayers of the Monks

t is not difficult to establish that the monk prays continually in the dark corners of the narthex as he attends the lengthy services. His only weapon and companion are his rosary and ceaseless prayer. The environment commands him. The quiet recitation of the psalms guides him. The gilded screens of the churches, the heavy silver 'perpetual' lamps, the imposing portable icons and the sacred forms portrayed on the walls glint in the trembling light of the candles and scatter endless irridescence.

The Canonarch, who in his impressive attire is reminiscent of an unparalleled Doric simplicity, is the only moving shape among the spirits and the shadows of the devotional half-light. He moves noiselessly from one cantor to another to lead the chanting. The cantors in their turn sing unhurriedly and with devotion. This form has been followed for more than eight hundred years in every manifestation of the monks' religious life, with the result that this liturgical language has become a means of cleansing and purification. Through the constant liturgical fife the monk is raised above the created world, abandons any contact with created things and becomes united with the effulgence of the Godhead, as Dionysius the Areopagite puts it. Each one, depending in the degree of his spiritual development, overcomes the darkness of death, the fear of judgment and the abyss of Hell, at and directs his gaze exclusively towards 'Lord who will come again with glory'.

The Orthodox monk sees before him constantly God as the expression of boundless love and as the victim of the sacrifice of the Cross for the benefit of the human race. For this reason, his prayer begins with petitions. This petitionary prayer is uneasy and full of cares and fears, but this is only a preparation for the true 'spiritual prayer'. It is, we would say, a gradual progress towards God, an attempt to approach Him, a spiritual quest. Gradually, as the soul gains in concentration and recollection, particular petitions disappear; they seem pointless, since God answers prayer in showing His providence in everything which surrounds him. The monk ceases to ask, since he trusts the will of God entirely. This state is called 'pure prayer'. The working together of the two co-operating wills continues through all the stages of the ascent of the monk to God.

Thus at some point the monk leaves the natural sphere and the spirit alone is active, all movement comes to a stop and prayer ceases. This is perfect peace, unique calm. This is the exultation of the spirit which has found its peace which is called 'ecstacy', since the monk 'steps outside' himself and does not known whcthcr he is in this life or that which is to come.

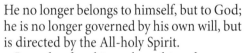

He no longer belongs to himself, but to God; he is no longer governed by his own will, but is directed by the All-holy Spirit.

In order for this to be achieved, prayer must be as continual and unceasing as breathing or the beating of the heart. It is to this art of prayer that the monks of Meteora are dedicated, as is every Orthodox monk.

The Visitors and the Monks

A visit to the monasteries of Meteora suggests a comparison. The visiting pilgrims are completely preoccupied with external beauty, with the delights of the life of nature, without taking a single step in the direction of learning the secrets of the soul of the monks. These ascetics, cut off as they are from the world, find the truth only through this very solitude. The pilgrims admire only the beauties of nature, without the life of the monks being for them a step of initiation, and they are left only with the simple pleasure of the senses. Thus they return to the world without getting to know the way of life of the monks at all.

THE MONASTERY OF THE TRANSFIGURATION
THE GREAT METEORO

The rock on which the Monastery of the Transfiguration of Christ is built is at the western end of the 'stone forest' and is the largest in the area. The rock is 613 metres above sea level and 415 above the bed of the Peneus, while the area on top where the monastery stands is of about 50,000 square metres. The height of the rock on the side from which we ascend is 250 metres, while 115 steep and irregular steps lead to the entrance to the monastery, which is known as the Great Meteoro. The suspended rope ladders are today no longer used and the net hauled up from the specially constructed winching house now conveys only goods and very occasionally pious visiting monks. As we go up the steps, we see first on the left the hermitage of the founder of the Monastery of St. Athanasius, a small simple building completely buried in the rock. Continuing the climb, we arrive at the monastery. Until 1923 the ascent was made by successive rope ladders and the net. Afterwards dark passages and steps were cut in the rock and so today the visitor reaches the monastery easily. The first buildings which we see are the tower with the winch, the bakery and various cells.

The Katholikon.

The finest building of the monastery is the central church, which is termed the Katholikon and is dedicated to the Transfiguration of Christ. Grand and impressive it stands in the centre of the complex of buildings and is 42 metres long and 24 metres high. From an architectural point of view, it is a cruciform domed church with a twelve sided dome set on a drum. The Katholikon is divided into ante-narthex, narthex, nave and sanctuary and is an excellent example of the second and third periods of Byzantine architecture.

The sanctuary, which in former times was the first katholikon of the monastery, is a small, cruciform domed two-columned church which lost its narthex when the new church was built. Ten metres long, it was built before 1382 by the founder of the Monastery of St. Athanasius. Later (1388) it was added to by Joasaph and was decorated with murals in 1484. A relevant inscription on the eastern wall of the sanctuary above the lavabo, where it seems that at one time there was a door, states:

THIS HOLY AND SACRED CHURCH OF OUR LORD AND GOD JESUS CHRIST WAS RAISED AND BUILT FROM THE FOUNDATIONS BY THE LABOUR AND AT THE EXPENSE OF OUR MOST BLESSED FATHERS ATHANASIUS AND JOASAPH IN THE YEAR 1388. THE FOUNDERS WERE COMMEMORATED BY THE EFFORTS AND LABOUR OF THE LEAST OF THE BRETHREN IN 1484, INDICTION 2, 9 NOVEMBER.

The Monastery of the Transfiguration
(The Greata Meteoro).

The Monastery of the Transfiguration. Drawing by B. Barskij, 1745.

The main body of the church is well lit and covered with paintings. It can be established from inscriptions andother sources and other sources that it was built and decorated in 1552, in the time of the extremely active Abbot Symeon.

The screen of the Katholikon, which is of exceptionally fine workmanship, is carved from wood and gilded. It was made in 1791 and depicts plant and animal motifs. Below the cross which surmounts the screen and above the Beautiful Gate is the following inscription:

PARTHENIUS BEING ABBOT THE WORK OF THE HANDS OF CONSTANTINE ANATOPITIS AND COSTAS METSOVITIS 1791 AUGUST 6.

Below this inscription and around the Beautiful Gate another states that in 1635 the monks of the monastery paid for the construction of the Beautiful Gate and that the name of the craftsman was Ioannis. Other inscriptions on the screen mention the Archpriest Paisios and the Abbot Parthenius, in whose time the screen was constructed. The icons on the screen are of fine workmanship and are executed in egg tempura. The famous method of using soot was employed in some of them. The episcopal throne, of wood, was made in 1617 and is decorated with representations from the plant kingdom. These are in mother-of-pearl and ivory and employ the 'inlay' technique. There are also two wooden lecterns with various mother-of-pearl and ivory designs. On one of these it is recorded that they were made in the time of the Abbot Parthenios, Kallinikos being the Chief Cantor.

The narthex of the Katholikon with its nine small cupolas is spacious and is supported by four columns. At the back, to the right, is the tomb of the founders Joasaph and Athanasius, who are depicted above holding a monastery in their hands. The ante-narthex is also large and is decorated with a few murals and 'tryvlia' — that is, plates with various designs. The entrance to the main church is in the centre of the ante-narthex. Low down to the left of he entrance is the following inscription:

THIS HOLY AND SACRED CHURCH OF THE TRANSFIGURATION OF OUR LORD JESUS CHRIST WAS RAISED AT THE EXPENSE AND BY THE LABOURS OF THE ASSEMBLED BRETHREN IN THE YEAR 1544/5.

Plan of the Katholikon of the Great Meteoro, by G. Sotiriou.

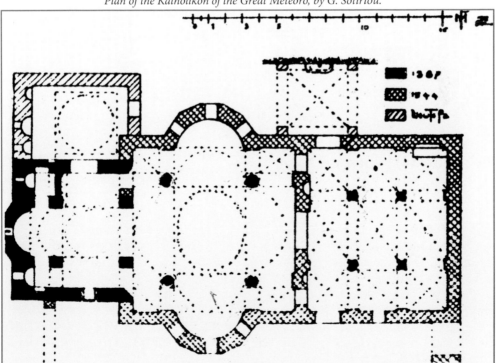

The Nativity. Portable icon, 16th century

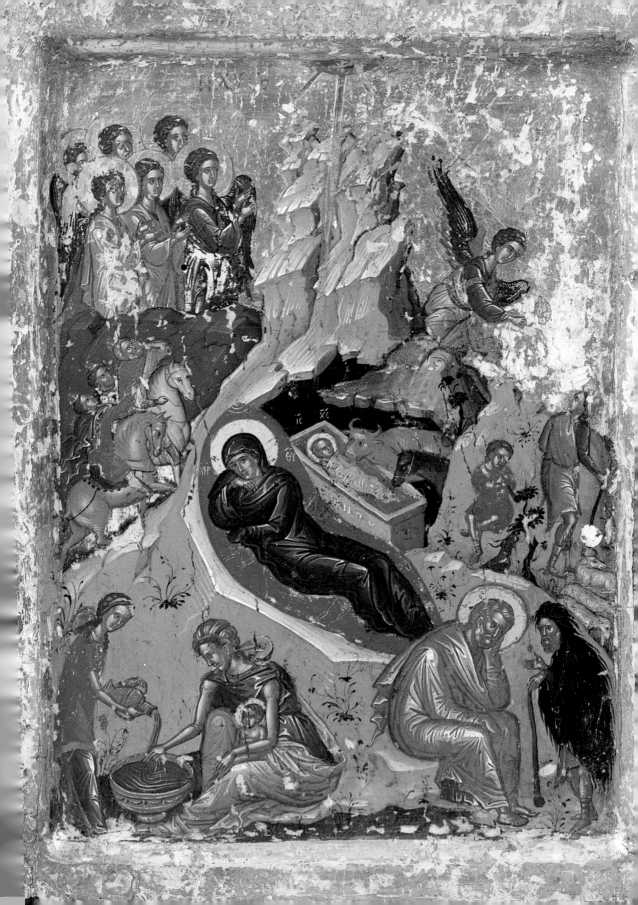

The Murals

The church is covered with icon compositions drawn both from the doctrinal and the liturgical cycle of the Orthodox Church. These compositions are characterized by powerful artistic inspiration, skill and plasticity. Their design is distinguished by a feeling for colour and the rendering of detail. The graphic decoration of the sanctuary is particularly fine, the scenes depicted, like the others in the church, are the work of an experienced icon-painter. The icons in the body of the church, as well as those in the narthex, with their famous representations of the martyrdoms of the saints, show artistic fervour and expressiveness. Unfortunately we do not know who the artist was. Expert opinion is not in complete agreement, but tends towards the conclusion that 'the murals in the Katholikon of Meteora (i.e. of the Transfiguration) must be the last work of the famous Cretan icon-painter Theophanis'.

Apart from the Katholikon, the Monastery of the Great Meteoro has three other smaller churches built at different dates. The first is that of St. John the Baptist. It has a carved wooden screen and murals belonging to the 16th century. Next is the Church of Sts. Constantine and Helen, which also has a carved wooden screen and was built in 1789. It has no murals. An inscription recording its building is built into the wall at the entrance to the monastery.

The sufferings of the Saints (16th century).

The first Ecumenical Synod. Mural.

Refectory - Museum

When the monastery had a large number of monks, they made use of the spacious refectory which has now been converted into a museum. This ancient rejectory of the monastery has been preserved in very good condition. It has a length or 35m. and is 12m. broad. Five columns support the ceiling, which is formed into four single and two double domes decorated with zig-zags and other —chiefly geometrical— designs. In the niche of the refectory there is an icon of the Virgin between the angels Gabriel and Michael. An iscription to the right of the entrance informs the visitors:

THIS REFECTRORY WAS BUILT FROM THE FOUNDATIONS BY THE EFFORTS AND LABOUR OF THE ASSEMBLED BRETHREN AND AT THE EXPENSE OF THE ABBOT MASTER SYMEON, MONK, IN THE MONTH OF AUGUST 1557.

The refectory, with its area of 190 sq. m., has now been converted into a museum and houses valuable relics, works which needed great patience and persistence. Among the relics exhibited for the visitor's admiration are: crucifixes and their holders, Easter sepulchres and icons, chalices and Gospels, episcopal pastoral staffs and vestments, iconographic and miniature work, golden bulls, seals, lead bulls and other documents of great historical and artistic value. We would particularly draw atention to a carved wooden crucifix, the work of the monk Daniel, which took ten years to carve. On only one of its sides it has ten scenes with several figures each and 24 representations of single figures. Among the many important portable icons of great value we would mention the Humiliation, the Virgin Mourning, Doubting Thomas, the Evangelists etc.

Behind the refectory is the infirmary of the monastery.

MONASTERY OF ALL SAINTS VARLAAM

History

The Monastery of Varlaam is built on a lofty rock in the 'stone forest' of Meteora at a height of 373 m. First to live on the rock was the monk Varlaam, who, around the year 1350, built some cells there together with a church dedicated to the Three Hierarchs. Later the brothers Nectarios and Theophanis went up onto this rock and in 1518 rebuilt on the ruins of the older buildings the church of the Three Hierarchs and a little later the churches of All Saints and St. John the Baptist. These two brothers came from the noble family of Apsarades of Ioannina — as we are informed by surviving inscriptions.

The first ascetic ascended the rock by a system of successive scaffoldings supported on beams wedged into holes in the rocks. His example was followed by others, and the result was the building of the monasteries of Meteora.

The scaffolding was later replaced by long rope ladders, which produced vertigo in the climbers. Those who did not dare to ascend by the rope ladders were hauled up in a net. The ascent took half an hour of worry and terror. Every visitor broke out in a cold sweat as the net, leaving terra firma, swung in the void with a circular movement, while the winch creaked, threatening to send him at any moment into the abyss.

In 1923, 195 steps were cut in the same rock; these now lead the visitor to the top comfortably and safely. The net is still used today for foodstuffs and other necessities for the upkeep of the monastery.

The Katholikon

The most impressive building of the Varlaam monastery is the central church or Katholikon. A large building, it is dedicated to All Saints. From an architectural point of view, it is a cruciform, domed, four-columned composite like, that is, the Katholika of the monasteries on Mount Athos. It consists of narthex, nave and sanctuary. The church, as one document relates, was built in twenty days, the materials having been collected on top of the rock over a period of 22 years. It is also related that the proprietor himself, Theophanis, who had been bed-ridden for 10 whole months, as soon as he was told that the work had been finished, rose from his bed of pain and when, with the help of a stick, he went to the church and saw it completed, he raised his hands and praised God, at the same time giving thanks to all the saints. Immediately afterwards —the account continues— he blessed the monks, the stone-quarriers, the builders, the masons and the craftsmen and, returning full of joy to his cell, then died. An inscription concerning the building of the Katholikon can be found in the southern part of the nave and reads as follow:

THIS SACRED AND VENERABLE CHURCH OF THE REVERED MONASTERY OF ALL SAINTS WAS RAISED FROM THE FOUNDATIONS BY THE MOST HOLY AMONG THE MONKS AND BRETHEREN MASTER NECTARIOS AND MASTER THEOPHANIS IN THE YEAR 1548 AND WAS RESTORED IN 1780.

On pages 44-45 the Varlaam Monastery (All Saints).
A narrow footpath with many steps leads to the monastery building.

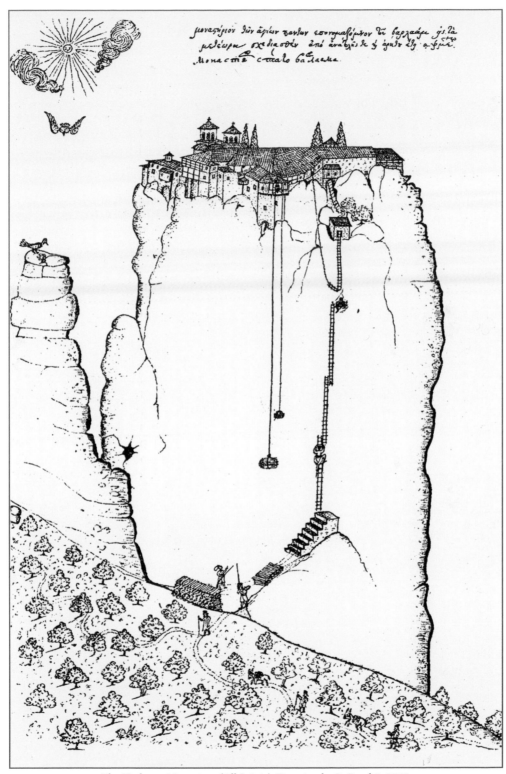

The Varlaam Monastery (All Saints). Drawing by B. Barskij, 1745.

The screen of the Katholikon is carved from wood and depicts scenes from the plant and animal kingdoms. The episcopal and abbatial throne, the shrine and lectern decorated with mother-of-pearl and ivory mosaic in various patterns give a particular splendour to the church. The fact that the church was built by the brothers Nectarios and Theophanis can be read in two other inscriptions to be found in the sanctuary. The first is on the outside of the sanctuary and the second on the window of the niche.

The narthex is spacious and contains, apart from its excellent murals, the tomb of the proprietors Nectarios and Theophanis. The tomb was originally carved out, by the proprietors themselves, in the chapel of the Three Hierarchs and was transferred later to the Katholikon. An explanatory inscription in the north-eastern portico of the narthex, where the Virgin is shown full length, reads:

THE NARTHEX OF THE CHURCH OF ALL SAINTS WAS DECORATED WITH THE AID AND AT THE EXPENSE OF THE BISHOP OF VELLA BELOVED OF GOD, MASTER ANTONIOS APSARAS OF IOANNINA, IN THE YEAR 1566 AND IN THE YEAR 1780 AND THE YEAR 1782 ALL THE DECORATION OF THE SANCTUARY OF THE KATHOLIKON AND OF THIS NARTHEX WAS RESTORED BY THE AID AND AT THE EXPENSE OF THE HUMBLE OF STAGI, PARTHENIOS, IN MEMORIAM AND FOR THE SALVATION OF HIS SOUL.

A second inscription on the north side of the narthex gives further information about the decoration of the church, which was carried out by the priest Georgios and his brother Frankos in 1566.

The Murals

he wealth of murals in the Katholikon includes compositions drawn from the historical, dogmatic and liturgical cycle of the Orthodox Church.

The wallpaintings are characterized by artistic skill and plasticity. The rich decoration of the main body of the church shows realism and the influence of Italian originals.

By sharp contrasts of light and darkness, the icon-painter of the Katholikon of the Varlaam Monastery shows, with every detail, all the phases of an event, a fact which shows that he borrowed features from Western models in the execution, chiefly, of his representations which contain a number of figures. In the portrayal of single saints he followed Orthodox tradition, since Western art had no such models to offer.

Today it is accepted by scholars the decoration of the main body of the Katholikon of the Varlaam Monastery was carried out by the great icon-painter Frankos Katelanos, who in the year 1560 was working at the Monastery of Megisti Lavra on Mount Athos. Katelanos was one of the most important icon-painters of the 16th century. In spite of the fact that he tried to make his work show originality, the influence on him of Theophanis, who decorated the church of the Monastery of St. Nicholas Anapafsas a few years before, can be seen.

St Catherine, Barbara and Thecla. Wall painting, 1627.

The icons in the narthex, according to inscriptions, supported by other comparisons and testimonies, are the work of the priest George Dikotaris, Ecclesiarch of Thebes, and Frankos Dikotaris.

Apart from the Katholikon at the Varlaam monastery, there is also the chapel of the Three Hierarchs. This is a single-nave church with carved wooden screen and excellent murals. The restoration of this chapel, as recorded on a tile incorporated into the wall there, took place in 1627. On its north wall there is the following inscription:

THIS CHAPEL OF THE THREE HIERARCHS, BASIL THE GREAT, GREGORY THE THEOLOGIAN, AND JOHN CHRYSOSTOM WAS RAISED FROM THE FOUNDATIONS AND DECORATED BY THE MOST BLESSED MONKS AND BROTHERS OF THE HOLY AND VENERABLE MONASTERY OF ALL SAINTS WHILE CYRIL AND SERGIUS WERE ABBOTS OF THE MONKS AND BRETHREN IN THE YEAR 1627, AND WAS DECORATED BY THE HAND OF THE SINNER IOANNIS, PRIEST, WITH HIS CHILDREN IN THE YEAR 1627, INDICTION 9, FROM STAGI.

Among the other buildings which the visitor can see are the old refectory, the infirmary, the hospice for the aged and the chapel of Sts. Cosmas and Damian.

The old refectory has been converted into a sacristy. Among the relics which are preserved there are fine miniatures, holy sepulchre cloths, episcopal vestments, elaborate carved wooden crucifixes, portable icons, eucharistic vessels and many other objects. Particularly noteworthy is a manuscript Gospel Book of the Byzantine Emperor Constantine Porphyrogenne containing the Emperor's own signature.

The Blessed Sisois at the tomb of Alexander the Great. Mural of the Katholikon.

'And wine, that maketh glad the heart of man...'

ROUSANOU MONASTERY

History

The Rosanou Monastery stands south east of the Great Meteoro between the monasteries of Varlaam and Holy Trinity on a vertical, hard, steep rock of the Stone Forest. As the visitor traverses the foot of this huge monolith, he is overwhelmed by a sense of awe as his eye takes in the almost sheer sides both of the rock and of the monastery. The monastery itself stands proudly on the summit of the rock on a platform barely big enough for it.

Until 1897 the ascent to the monastery was by rope ladders. Later two wooden bridges served both monks and visitors. Since 1936 two strong, picturesque bridges from the side of the mountain, which reduce the height of the rock, serve the same purpose. The cost of erecting the bridges was borne by Miss Daphne Baka of Kastraki.

As to the name of the Rousanou Monastery, the available information is insufficient for us to reach firm conclusions. It would seem, however, the name Rousanou or Rosano is to be traced to the founder, who was called Rousanos. Others maintain that the first proprietor was from the village of Rosana in Thessaly and that this is the reason why the monastery was called Rousanou. Historical sources which are yet to be confirmed state that the Rousanou Monastery was founded in 1288 by the monks Nicodemus and Benedict. What is certain is that 156 years later the monastery was restored, the ruined buildings were rebuilt and the monastery started to operate as a community as a result of the efforts of the monks Maximus and Joasaph, who came from Ioannina in 1545. The monastery, according to our sources, began

to function again with the blessing of the then Metropolitan of Larissa Bessarion (ob. 1541) and the consent of the Abbot of the Monastery of the Great Meteoro.

The Katholikon

The church of the monastery, that is, the Katholikon, is dedicated to the Transfiguration of Christ. From an architectural point of view it a domed, three-apsed Byzantine church, decorated with excellent murals drawn from the historical, doctrinal and liturgical cycle of the Orthodox Church. The compositions, which show plasticity and grace, are the work of an experienced astist. The screen is of gilded carved wood, while the shrine of the Virgin has various patterns in mother-of-pearl.

The construction of the shrine was paid for by the monks Damascenus and Bessarion, as a relevant inscription informs us, and is the work of the priest Rizos.

The murals, which, as the inscription states, were executed in 1561 at the expense of the Abbot Arsenius, are, even after the passage of 400 years, in a very good state of preservation.

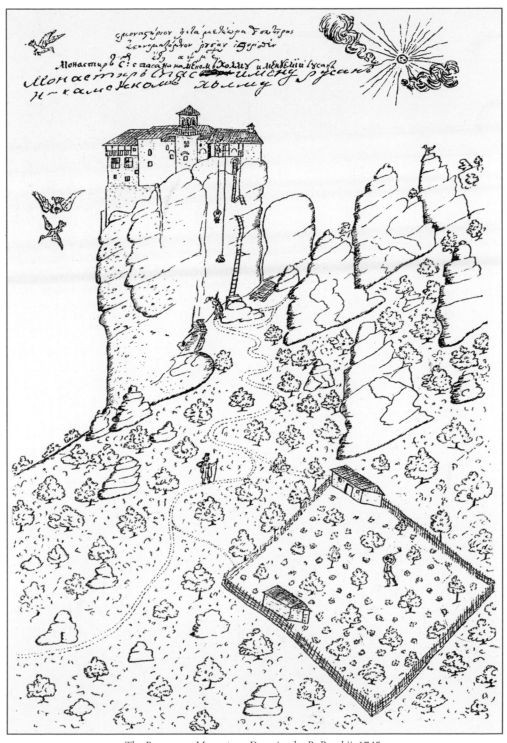

The Rousanou Monastery. Drawing by B. Barskij, 1745.

HOLY TRINITY MONASTERY

The Monastery of the Holy Trinity is built on a lofty rock of unusual shape to the north east of the Monastery of St. Stephen. One hundred and forty steps carved in the rock lead you in safety to the summit on which the monastery stands. Experts maintain that the Holy Trinity monastery is the third oldest among the religious houses of Meteora. It can be established from inscriptions and other evidence that the main church, that is, the Katholikon, was built in 1476, while the narthex is of later date. The external construction of the walls, monograms in tiles etc. point to around the 14th century as the date of the foundation of the monastery.

The narthex, however, was built in 1689 and decorated in 1692. It is highly probable that the monastery was built within the space of 18 years, i.e. between 1458 and 1476, as we are assured by the historical sources and various travellers who visited the monasteries of Meteora at various periods. We do not know yet whether the report which represents the monk Dometios as the original founder is absolutely correct. Tradition, however, maintains that it took seventy whole years to convey the materials up to the top of the rock before building started.

The Katholikon

The Monastery of the Holy Trinity has two churches — the central one, known as the Katholikon and the chapel of St. John the Baptist. The Katholikon, which is not a large structure, is dedicated to the Holy Trinity. Architecturally, it is a two-columned cruciform domed church. The building construction of the eastern part of the sanctuary is particulary carefully executed. A pseudo-trefoil window adorns the apse and has toothed brick decorations with crosses and monograms of Christ (IE. XP. NIKA). A double line of toothed bricks follows round the whole of this side under the window and lends particular grace to the structure of the church. On the south face of the church two inscriptions are incorporated into the wall, one next to the other, which state:

IN THE YEAR 1476 AND BY THE HAND OF THE MONK NICODEMUS AND PTOCHOS RAKENDYTOS.

Another inscription dealing with the decoration of the church is inside the narthex. This informs us in detail of those who paid and of those who took charge not only at the foundation, but also at the decoration of the church.

The screen of the Katholikon is of carved wood, gilded and decorated with various representations drawn from the plant kingdom. It has remarkable portable icons. The icon of Christ, painted in 1662, which can be found there, represents Christ in local (Karagouniko) costume. Another portable icon shows the Holy Trinity symbolically, that is, by the scene of the three angels.

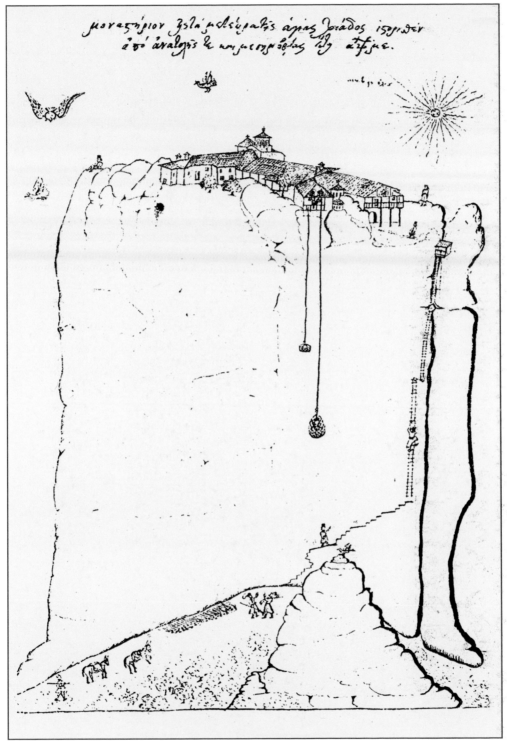

The Holy Trinity Monastery. Drawing by B. Barskij, 1745.

The Murals

he church is full of various iconographic compositions belonging to the historical, doctrinal and liturgical cycle of the Orthodox Church. These are murals of exceptional quality, which are characterized by true artistic spirit. A revelant inscription, apart from the one referred to above, dealing with the decoration of the church is to be found inside on the north wall.

The inscription tells us, among other things, that the murals of the main church were executed by the brothers Antonios, priest, and Nicolas in 1741.

The other church which has been preserved up to the present in the Monastery of the Holy Trinity is that of St. John the Baptist. This is a chapel in the form of a rotonda carved in the rock. It is the first thing which the visitor of the monastery comes upon. A relevant inscription concerning the building of the chapel can be found on the internal door lintel. This states that it was built by the labours and at the expense of the monks Damascenus, Jonah and Parthenios.

Finally, the view from the Holy Trinity monastery is unrivalled. To the east is the Monastery of St. Stephen, to the west the monasteries of Varlaam and the Great Meteoro and to the south Kalambaka. The top of the rock has an area of approximately one hectare, and on it there are, besides the churches which we have described, the cells of the monks, the kitchen, the refectory, two cisterns and a little cultivable land.

The screen of the Church of Holy Trinity.

THE MONASTERY OF ST. STEPHEN

History

s you approach Kalambaka from the direction of Trikkala and look towards the Meteora rocks, you will see high up on the first rock on the right, where it has stood proudly for centuries, the Monastery of St. Stephen. The deep green of the often tranquil and peaceful Thessalian plain and the greyish yellow of the dark sheer masses of the stone forest blend here in unprecedented harmony. It seems as though hundreds of sheer rocks have set off on a race and that someone has held them back in mid-air severed from the mountain which connects them and naked of the greenery which luxuriates around them. On the summit of these steep rocks, some 800 years ago, were built monasteries which startle us with their appearance and impress us with their mass. From Kalambaka the monasteries seem like phenomena in the heavens which have taken off from the earth heavenwards with overwhelming grandeur.

The Monastery of Saint Stephen can be reached by two paths. One is from the village of Kastraki and the other from the south-easterly part of Kalambaka. As you approach, you see a spacious and untrodden ancient castle waiting to receive you, built on the top of a gigantic rock with an area of 7,500 square metres. In former times, as can be seen from works of art, plans and engravings at the Monastery of St. Stephen, access to the monastery was easier than to the others, thanks to a movable bridge which connected the rock

on which the monastery stands with the hill of Koukoulas opposite. Today a permanent eight-metre bridge leads one in safety to the entrance to the monastery.

An inscription on the lintel of the entrance used to testify, until a few years ago, that the monastery was built in 1192 — a fact which is confirmed by historians and scholars. The inscription, no longer in place, used to read:

ST. JEREMIAH

According to the inscription, the place was first inhabited before 1200 A.D. and the first prior of the hermitage was Jeremiah. At the beginning of the 14th century we are told that the monastery was coenobitic i.e. the monks lived a common life. In 1333 the Byzantine Emperor Andronikos Palae-ologos (1328-1341) arrived in Thessaly and received hospitality at the monastery. The result of this was that he made many generous gifts to the then abbot and the monks. From that date the monastery acquired the privilege of being designated 'royal'. In 1350 the church of St. Stephen was built. We hear that the proprietors of the monastery were the Blessed Theophilus of Siataina and Antony Katakouzenos, son of a Serbian noble. In 1398 the Lord of Hungro — Wallachia, Ioannis Vladislavos, donated to the monastery a piece of the True Cross, relics of John the Baptist, property in Rumania and other benefits, while his nephew, Vornikos Dragoumaris, gave the monastery the head of St. Charalambos. In 1545 the Patriarch of Constantinople Jeremiah proclaimed the monastery a stavropegion, while in 1605 the

Patriarch Raphael calls it 'royal, self-governing, patriarchal and a stavropegion'. In 1798, when Paisios was Bishop of Stagi and Ambrose abbot the imposing central Church of St. Charalambos was built. In 1850 the monastery built the Constantine School of Kalambaka and donated approximately 80,000 gold drachmas for the building of a secondary school at Trikkala. In 1888 the Monastery had 31 monks, but by 1960 it was virtually deserted. In 1961 it was converted into a nunnery and today is in a flourishing condition. The above historical information is drawn from patriarchal chrysobulls, patriarchal bulls and other official documents and decisions.

μοναστήριον τȣ̃ ἁγίȣ ςεφάνȣ ῃς τὰ μετέωρα ἱςȣριωθὲν
ἀπὸ μέρȣς ἀρκτικȣ̃ῃ ἡ δοχη̃ȣ ἔῃς ατ̅φ̅μ̅ε̅.

ἥλιος ἀνατολικός
ὕπνος

The Monastery of St. Stephen. Drawing by B. Barskij, 1745.

Gilded crosses. Treasury of the monastery of St. Stephen.

Gold embroidered Good Friday bier cloth (1857).

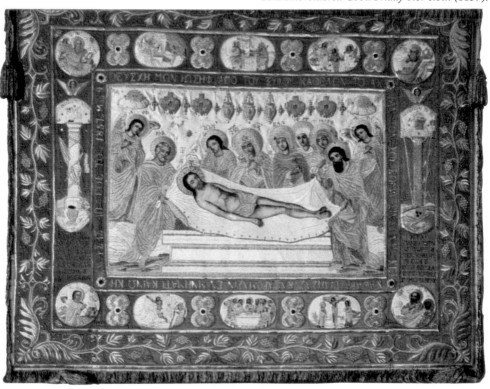

Wood carving on shrine. Monastery of St. Stephen, 1836.

The Katholikon

Spacious and imposing, the central church of the monastery, that is, the Katholikon, is dedicated to St. Charalambos. Architecturally it is a cruciform domed church with three apses, four columns, narthex, credence table and sacristy, exactly like the churches of the monasteries of Mount Athos. It was built in 1798, while parts of it have undergone restoration from time to time, as in 1868, 1902 and 1915, as the relevant inscriptions testify. On the outside on the pronarthex on the left side of the choir there are three inscriptions, the middle one of which has the longest text. The first on the right refers to the building of the church in the time of Paisios, Bishop of Stagi, and the abbot Ambrose.

The central insription is concerned with a prayer of Paisios, Bishop of Stagi, for the church, the brotherhood and his own soul, asking God not to forget him on the terrible Day of Judgment. The third inscription, the first on the left, that is, again refers to the founding of the church and mentions those chiefly responsible for the work.

The narthex is a simple one and is supported by four columns. In the pronarthex there is an inscription which mentions the benefactors responsible for the foundation. In the inscription the outer narthex is called Apoltaria and we are told that its construction was paid for by the Abbot Theophanis, the fathers of the monastery and those who were staying in the monastery at the time of building.

The church is not decorated with painted icons. A fine carved wooden ciborium stands over the altar. The screen of the church is also of carved wood and is of excellent workmanship. The carving deals with symbolic themes drawn from the plant and animal kingdoms as well as remarkable compositions showing the Last Supper, St. Demetrius, St. Stephen the Protomartyr, St. George, etc. A carved inscription over the icon of St. Charalambos reads:

THE SCREEN OF THE CHURCH OF ST. CHARALAMBOS WAS MADE AT THE EXPENSE OF THE BISHOP OF STAGI, MASTER GABRIEL, THE MONK MASTER THEOPHANIS FROM SOULATENA TRIKKI, BEING ABBOT, BY THE HAND OF MASTROCOSTAS AND

DIMITRI FROM THE VILLAGES OF METSOVO IN THE YEAR 1814.

The episcopal throne and the shrines are also of carved wood, as is confirmed by an inscription of 1836, also of carved wood, which is on one of the shrines below the icon of the Virgin. Another inscription on another carved wooden shrine in the main church deals with the icons of the shrines and screen, which were executed in 1846.

Finally we should also mention the two lecterns which have various stylized representations in inlaid mother-of-pearl and ivory. At the entrance to the narthex on the outside there are stone carvings which have symbolic representations showing the vine, Latin crosses, double-headed eagles, cypresses etc. In the centre of the floor of the main church, carved in the middle of a circle is the double-headed eagle, eternal symbol of the powerful Byzantine empire.

The Church of St. Stephen the Protomartyr

part from the Katholikon of the monastery which we have described, there is also the old church of St. Stephen, which stands on the south-eastern part of the rock. This is a stone-built timbered structure with a single nave and a narthex. It measures 12 metres by five. The church is decorated with murals of the year 1501, as a relevant inscription states. Researchers, however, maintain that the inscription refers only to the icon of the Dormition of the Virgin and that the other murals are older.

Apart from the churches which we have described, the monastery has a refectory, guest house, courtyard and the cells of the nuns. The refectory has been converted Into a sacristy where the visitor can admire fine carved wooden crosses, gold-decorated Gospel books, chalices, censers, port-

able icons of splendid workmanship, gold-embroidered vestments, sepulchre cloths, manuscript codices with miniatures, other liturgical vessels and belts involving much detailed, patient work. In the southern part of the monastery is the guest house for the entertainment of visitors.

Today Byzantine icon-painting and music are cultivated here, with remarkable results. Some nuns engage most fruitfully in writing, while others with a university education (doctors, teachers etc.) concern themselves systematically with social monasticism. Thus the Monastery of St. Stephen at Meteora has proved to be a spiritual hive, making a valuable Orthodox Christian and social contribution in an age of uncertainties.

MONASTERY OF
ST. NICHOLAS ANAPAFSAS

History

South-west of the rocks of Meteora, near the village of Kastraki, among the ruined monasteries of Aghia Moni, the Almighty, John the Baptist and Doubiani, stands the Monastery of St. Nicholas Anapafsas. Many explanations, more or less peculiar, have been offered of the name Anapafsas, but the most likely is that it is the name of the person at whose expense the monastery, perhaps the oldest building, which is believed to have stood on the same site, was built.

The monastery which is preserved today was built around the close of the 15th century on the ruins —so the experts maintain— of an older one. Architectural considerations, however, and the remains of murals support the view that the church is of the 13th or 14th century. The narrow and confined surface of the rock on which the monastery stands is the reason why its various parts do not extend horizontally by are built on different levels, one above the other. Thus as we go up there, we find on the first level the church and refectory and on the second the cells of the monks. Everything about the place gives a sense of confinement and a feeling of mystery.

The Monastery of St. Nicholas Anapafsas today.

The Katholikon

The central church of the monastery is dedicated to St. Nicholas and is situated on the first level. It is long and narrow and attached at an angle to the southern part of the wall of the monastery, which itself follows the irregular formation of the rock. It has a low dome which is without windows, since, as we have noted above, the second level of the monastery is above it. In contrast with the body of the church, the narthex is relatively spacious and well-lit. However, this relative spaciousness of the narthex is not due to the large number of monks, since we know from an old description of the monastery that there were ten cells for monks and quarters for the abbot. The size of the narthex is to be attributed, it seems, to another cause — that is, that, since the monastery, because of the small surface area of the rock on which it is built, did not have a cloister, this narthex was used for the monks to sit there and study at times when there were no services going on in the main church or when they were not engaged in other activities. Thus this narthex served as the courtyard of the monastery. The church under discussion began to be built a few years before 1510, at the expense of the Metropolitian of Larissa Dionysios and the monk Nicanor, archpriest-exarch of Stagi (Kalambaka). The portraits of both these proprietors of the monastery are painted on the narthex of the church. The decoration of the church and narthex was finished in 1527, as we are informed by an inscription above the entrance to the church:

THE DIVINE AND VENERABLE CHURCH OF OUR FATHER AMONG THE SAINTS NICHOLAS WAS ERECTED FROM THE FOUNDATIONS BY HIS REVERENCE THE METROPOLITAN OF LARISSA MASTER DIONYSIOS AND THE MOST VENERABLE MONK NICANOR, EXARCH OF STAGI, AND THE BRETHREN ASSEMBLED AND WAS DECORATED AT THE EXPENSE OF THE WORTHLESS KYPRIANOS, 12 OF THE MONTH OF OCTOBER, BY THE HAND OF THE MONK THEOPHANIS OF STRELITZA IN CRETE. TOUPIKLIN BATHAS.

The Murals

The decoration of the walls was carried out by the monk Theophanis Strelitzas from Crete, who, in spite of the great difficulties caused by the narrowness of the space of the church, managed to present the whole of the rich iconographic scheme in the form which it had taken in the time of the Palealogues. There is no doubt that he was the most important icon-painter of the 16th century, who gave to Byzantine icon-painting its final form and who was followed not only by his own contemporaties but by later generations of icon-painters.

The compositions of the icons of the Katholikon at the Monastery of St. Nicholas Anapafsas are drawn from the historical, doctrinal and liturgical cycle of the Orthodox Church. This rich decoration of the church is marked by liveliness, originality, expressiveness and a luminosity of the bodies, which are portrayed against and dominate over a brown background, with the result that the individual compositions form a radiant whole. In a few words, we could say that the work of Theophanis, who is known to us by other major works on Mount Athos, is imbued by a powerful artistic spirit, skilled craftsmanship, plasticity and luminosity. We could draw attention particularly to the portrayal of the Virgin on the sanctuary, the Humiliation, the proprietors, the Dormition of the Blessed Ephraim, the Almighty, the Second Coming, the Temptation of Chirist and others. We append here the outlines of the life and work of the great Cretan icon-painter Theophanis Strelitzas.

The Monastery of St. Nicholas Anapafsas. Drawing by B. Barskij, 1745.

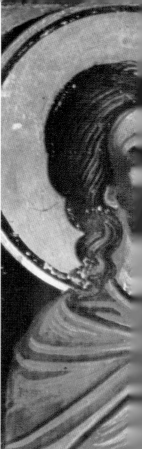

Icon composi
Anapafsas

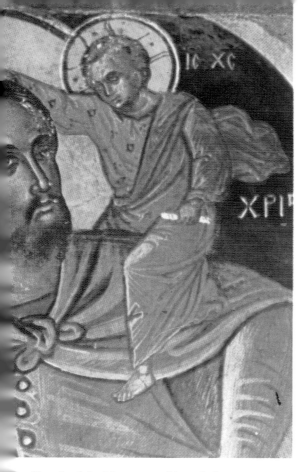

he Church of the Monastery of St Nicholas of Theophanis of Crete (16th century).

Christ tempted by the Devil. Mural of Theophanis, 1527.
(T. Provatakis, 'The Devil in Byzantine art', fig. 7).

Theophanis the Cretan must be placed in the first rank of Orthodox Christian icon-painters. The chief reresentative of the Cretan school, he was born around 1500 in Crete and worked in parts of Macedonia and Thrace, but principally at Mount Athos and Meteora. His surname was Strilitzas, but he was known as 'Bathas', as can be seen stated by his son Neophytos in an, inscription in the Cathedral of Kalambaka, which he decorated, together with the priest Kyriazis in 1573. Theophanis, a powerful artist, was initiated into the spirit of the Cretan school through murals, portable icons and designs. At Meteora, in 1527, he decorated the Katholikon of the Monastery of St. Nicholas Anapafsas and in 1535 carried out the painting of the walls of the Katholikon of the Lavra on Mount Athos. The year 1546 found him working at the Stavronikitas monastery on Mount Athos, assisted by his son Symeon. Without any doubt the works of Theophanis are characterized by nobility, spiritual depth, asceticism, expressiveness and idealism.

It is a form of art which remains close to Byzantine idealism. He liked conservatism, specific movements, the calm, the expression of internal emotion, the stylization of shapes and the high-lighting of the projecting features of the faces. He is not lacking in liveliness and his aim was the conveying of profound Orthodox truths; so that the faithful could pass from this material and passing world to the heavenly and eternal one. It is for precisely this reason that the essence of his work, consisting as it does in the expression of the heavenly and eternal spiritual world, ignores physical place and actual time. It operates within an ideal metaphysical location and in liturgical time. Nature in Byzantine art is presented in a supernatural manner. The mountains and hills are stylized, while plants and animals are portrayed geometrically. The design and the execution, as well as the gold background, show the efforts of the painters to distance their compostion from the world on earth. The body for the Orthodox painter is of secondary significance; for this reason he either covers it with garments in classical folds or presents it naked but dematerialized. Appearances —faces— are not presented in a beautified form, that is, with a beauty of this world. Rather, eschatological beauties are given to the appearance of the persons, and it is from this viewpoint that they are to be understood. Characteristic of this are the eyes, the forehead, the nose, the lips and the whole expression generally. The high forehead and the shape of the temples express the calm and tranquillity, the peace and blessedness which belong to the person thus portayed. The almond-shaped eyes, as a general rule, the thin and immaterial lips and the fine nose speak most expressively of the ideology of the representations and undoubtedly convey the heavenly blessedness of those who have become enslaved in good works to the true God. Thus the figures in the icons have always been examples and pointers in the right direction to the faithful in church. To sum up, one could say that this spiritual expression of the icon composistions both of the Cretan and the Macedonian schools is nothing other than the very greatness of Orthodox iconography. Theophanis died on 24 February in the year 1559.

Finally, other chapels at the Monastery of St. Nicholas Anapafsas are dedicated too St. Antony and St. John the Baptist.

The dormition of St Nicholas.

When you reach the stone forest of Meteora an involuntary sense of the sublime and beautiful overcomes you. The beautiful is there to be enjoyed and the sublime to be admired. The sense of the sublime manifests itself as a torrent of feelings seeking an outlet, while the sense of the beautiful through the resolving balance of struggling forces. The beautiful is expressed in proportion, since both its content and its form are in complete harmony and, consequently, a sense of Olympian serenity overtakes the observer. The sublime is intensified by the spectacle of the towering rocks, whose unique and hidden power can produce only awe and wonder. The concealed strength, brought to the surface by their peace, addresses itself to the soul and the feelings, while the beautiful affects the intelligence and the spirit.

And so, if you ever chance to be there as a pilgrim or as a visitor, you too will share in the sublime and the beautiful, as the fragrant breezes lap you, bringing you with them. Wafts of incense and the subdued chanting of monks in the surrounding monasteries. You would heave a sigh then of nostalgia, which remains without expression in the depths of your soul, as is always the case with the great experiences of life.

THE UNINHABITED AND RUINED MONASTERIES OF METEORA

part from the monasteries which are described above and which struggle to survive, at the same time serving society, there are also a number of uninhabited monasteries in the Meteora area. They are nearly all of them in ruins now and we know of their existence and the time of their prime both from manuscript codices and from the ruins which can be seen in various places in the stone forest of Meteora. Their existence can also be established from various engravings and works of art of various periods in the past. These monasteries are:

Monastery of St. George Mandilas

or the visitor to reach the Monastery of St. George Mandilas, now in ruins, he must make a laborious climb to a cave on a very high rock to the north east of the village of Kastraki. At the entrance to the cave even to-day hang kerchiefs ('mandilia') dedicated, in accordance with an ancient custom, by the inhabitants of Kastraki. The foundation of the monastery is placed in the 14th century, and perhaps it is one of the four monasteries built by the Prior of the Skete of Stagi Master Neilos, arount 1367. Today only a chapel carved in the rock has survived. An icon of St. George is to be found on the outside wall.

Monastery of St. Nicholas Batovas or Kofinas.

he half-ruined church of St. Nicholas Batovas is to be found in a cave between Kalambaka and the village of Kastraki at the spot called 'Kofinia'. In order to reach it, the visitor must pass through three caves linked by wooden ladders. The third ladder leads to the platform of the monastery, where the cistern for rain water, the winch used by the ascetics to haul up supplies, and for the monks themselves to ascend and the small chapel, literally carved out of the rock, are situated.

The monastery was probably founded in 1400. In the 15th century it is mentioned in the 'Syngramma Historikon', while in the 17th century it is referred to in the register preserved at the Great Meteoro (Transfiguration) monastery (Codex No. 372). On the lintel of the chapel the following inscription is preserved:

THIS MONASTERY OF ST. NICHOLAS BATOVAS WAS RESTORED THROUGH THE AID OF THE MONK IGNATIUS, WHO ONCE SERVED AT THE MONASTERY OF ST. STEPHEN AND LATER CAME HERE, 1876.

In 1943 the chapel was bombarded in the course of the war and was almost completely destroyed.

Monastery of the Holy Spirit

The ascent for the visitor to the Monastery of the Holy Spirit is somewhat difficult, as the rock on which it is built is more than 300 metres high. A narrow pathway carved in the steep rock leads to the chapel which remains to this day. The icons have been completely destroyed. The altar, the credence table and shrine are carved in the rock, while at the entrance on the right there is a carved sarcophagus which is the tomb of the proprietor.

On the left of the church are two cisterns which collect rain water in the winter. Scattered here and there are ruined cells and a very few wild trees. On the summit of the rock stands an iron cross which is, it is said, the cross erected by Stephen Dusan as a trophy.

Monastery of the Purification

The visitor who turns his eyes towards the stone forest today sees the Monastery of the Purification deserted and uninhabited in a steep cave among the rocks of Meteora. It was built in 1367 by the Prior of the Skete and Abbot of Doupiani. Today only the church remains. Architecturally this is a simple single-naved cruciform building. On its shorter sides there are niches, as well as two asymetrical blind arches, on the upper part of which there are windows admitting light to the church, which is decorated with icons. The iconographic compositions are concerned with the historical, doctrinal and liturgical cycle of the Orthodox Church. These are presented on one plane only without any unified scale of figures, as was the custom at the time with Eastern folk art, which took shape in the fourteenth century where it took on new elements from the art of the Palaeologues, that is, a picturesqueness, many architectural features etc, The screen of the church is of carved wood without icons. Near the screen Christ is portrayed standing, life-size, in sandals. With His right hand he gives a blessing and in His left he holds the book of the Gospel. This is Jesus Christ of the Ascension, to whom the church is dedicated, as can also be seen from an inscription to be found on the lintel which reads:

THE SACRED AND VENERABLE CHURCH OF THE ASCENSION OF OUR LORD AND SAVIOUR JESUS CHRIST WAS RAISED FROM THE FOUNDATIONS AND DECORATED BY THE AID AND AT THE EXPENSE OF THE MOST REVEREND MONK MASTER NEILOS, PRIOR OR THE SKETE OF STAGI AND ABBOT OF THE VENERABLE MONASTERY OF DOUBIANI, IN THE REIGN OF OUR WORSHIPFUL KING MASTER SYMEON PALAEOLOGOS OURESIS, EMPEROR OF THE ROMANS OF SERBIA AND RUMANIA HIS HOLINESS VESSAROS BEING BISHOP, IN THE SACRED.

It is clear from the inscription that the church was built in 1367, that is 6875 years from the creation of the world. At the end of the inscription it is noted that it was restored in 1765 by one Vlachavas, who can be none other than the famous warrior chief Athanasios Vlachavas.

Monastery of Palaiopanayia

This monastery is between the villages Vlachava and Asproklisia, near the Ionas (Mikani) tributary of River Peneus, in the Chasia area. All that remains today is a chapel decorated with icons carved out of rock and vaulted. It would appear that it is this monastery which is referred to in a decree of the Serbian Tsar Dusan in 1358 and of his brother Symeon in 1362 when they speak of 'the cave called that of Cyril in the place Mikani'. It is also referred to in a letter of the Bishop of Larissa Neophytos in 1541, as well as in the 'Register' at the Monastery of the Great Meteoro.

Monastery of the Holy Trinity

The rocks of Meteora and the Roussanou Monastery

Monastery of the Holy Trinity

Monastery of the Great Meteoron and Monastery of Varlaam

Monastery of Saint Nicolas Anapafsas

Monastery of Roussanou

Monastery of Roussan

Monastery of Varlaa...

The day of judgement (Varlaam Monastery)

The Martydom of Saints (Monastery of the Transfiguration)

Saint Varlaam and Saint Joasaph (Varlaam Monastery)

Monastery of the Transfiguration: The Baptism (14th century)

Holy Bishops Serving (16th cent. Monastery of the Transfiguration)

Saint Basil and Saint Athanasios of Alexandria (Monastery of the Transfiguration)

Skete of Doubiani

he Skete of Doubiani was situated north west of the site of the present-day village of Kastraki where today there is a simple and humble chapel to the Virgin. The ascetics of the retreat known as the Skete of Stagi lived in various caves in the surrounding rocks, where they prayed in tiny chapels called 'prosefchadia'. Each Sunday they would go down to a more central church which was called the 'Kyriakon' to celebrate the Liturgy. The church, according to written testimony, was dedicated to the Archangels Michael and Gabriel. The church which is preserved today is in good condition, as are some of its murals. An inscription preserved in a 16th century chronicle, relating to the building and decorating of four churches by the Prior of the Skete of Stagi and Abbot of Doubiani Master Neilos, reads:

ERECTED FROM THE FOUNDATIONS AND DECORATED BY THE AID AND AT THE EXPENSE OF THE MOST HONOURABLE MONK MASTER NEILOS, ABBOT OF THE VENERABLE AND HOLY MONASTERY OF THE ALL HOLY MOTHER OF GOD OF DOUBIANI AND PRIOR OF THE SKETE OF STAGI IN THE REIGN OF OUR MOST REVERED AND SERENE LORD SYMEON PALAEOLOGOS OURESIS, MASTER BESSARION OF STAGI, MOST BELOVED OF GOD, BEING BISHOP IN TRIKKI, IN THE YEAR 1367.

Monastery of the Holy Apostles

he Monastery of the Holy Apostles stood on the 'aias' rock above the present-day town of Kalambaka. Carved stairs, cisterns and the remains of murals can still be seen there. The monastery is referred to in a letter of the Bishop of Larissa Neophytos in 1551 and in the 'Register' in of 1650 which is kept today at the Monastery of the Great Meteoro (Transfiguration) under the name of 'Holy Apostles, known as Kallistou'. Perhaps the founder was called Kallistos, a name which is met with on the cover of an original Gospel book of the year 1547.

Monasteries of St. Gregory and St. Antony

alf-ruined outside railings and a section of a wooden hanging ladder are the only remains, on top of a steep rock, which testify to the existence of the Monastery of St. Gregory. On the same rock, exactly to the east of the ruins of this monastery, stood the Monastery of St. Antony. Of this only the church now remains in a satisfactory condition. Both monasteries belong to the 14th century.

Monastery of the Almighty

 ruined tower and sections of collapsed walls today bear witness to the existence of the Monastery of the Almighty on the northern part of the Doubiani rock. Proprietor of the monastery was the monk Neophytos, whose will, in a damaged and incomplete state, is preserved in the archives of the Great Meteoro. Also believed to have been proprietor of the monastery is the monk Serapion, its abbot in 1426, as we learn from the 'Syngramma Historikon'. The monastery is recorded first in the 'Register' of 1650.

Monastery of St. John the Baptist

he site of the Monastery of St. John Baptist was near to that of the Monastery of St. Nicholas Anapafsas on a very high road where there are ruins to the present day. It was on this rock that the Blessed Athanasios of Meteora took up residence in the beginning and where the proprietors of Varlaam, Theophanis and Nectaries, stayed for seven whole years before building their monastery. The monastery is known to us from manuscript codices and from a report sent to the Voivoid Ioannis Vassilios, Prince of Moldowallachia round about 1634-1653.

Ayia Moni

he site of Ayia Moni was below the rocks of the monasteries of Varlaam and the Great Meteoro. It was dedicated to the Virgin. We know of the monastery from written evidence and from a bull of the Ecumenical Patriarch Timotheos of the year 1614, in which, among other things, it is stated that more than 20 priest-monks and monks, who are listed by name, had been responsible for building from the foundations a small monastery, dedicated to the Virgin, in the place called 'Sterna' near the Varlaam monastery. They sought from the Patriarchate, moreover, that the monastery should be declared a 'stavropegion'.

Monastery of the Highest or of the Calligraphers

imself a brilliant and painstaking calligrapher, the monk Neilos wrote, in 1407, the history of his monastery —the 'Highest'— and he gives us abundant information about its foundation. It was called the Calligraphers' Monastery because there was there a workshop for copying and calligraphy which produced important manuscript codices, some of which survive today. The founder of the monastery was Paschalis of Kalambaka, who built it in 1347. Among his more important successors were the priest-monks Makarios, Neophytos, Dorotheos, Barnabas etc. Today all that remains are the ruins, which are to be found on a gigantic rock south east of the rock on which the Monastery of the Great Meteoro stands.

Monastery of St. Modestos

he Monastery of St. Modestos was on a very high rock opposite the Monastery of the Holy Trinity. It is known to us from a letter of the 12th century in which reference is made to the 'land of St. Modestos'. There is further mention of the monastery in the 'Register' in 1650 and in a bull of the Patriarch Timotheos in 1614. Today only ruins remain.

Monastery of the Veneration of St. Peter's Chains

he monastery built on a huge rock above Kalambaka known as 'Altsos' was known by the name of 'Alysos'. The probable date of its erection is 1400. In the 'Register', written in 1650, it is listed thirteenth among the monasteries of Meteora.

Monastery of St. Demetrius

oday it is difficult for the visitor to make the ascent to the Monastery of St. Demetrius, which is on the same rock as the Monastery of the Purification, to the east of it. There is evidence that it was one of the four most ancient monasteries of Meteora, built by the Prior of the Skete of Stagi, Master Neilos, in 1367.

It is mentioned in a report on monasteries to the Voivoid of Moldowallachia, Ioannis Vassilios (1634-1653). In 1788 the Bishop of Stagi and the monks of Varlaam, who used it as a dependent monastery, ceded it to the Monastery of the Purification, with a view to building cells for the monks, who had increased in number.

In 1809 the warrier-chief Papathymios Vlachavas who had made the monastery his headquarters was arrested by Ali Pasha, who completely destroyed it.

The church of the Dormition of the Virgin at Kalambaka.

KALAMBAKA

History

alambaka is 21 km. distant from Trikkala and five from the monasteries of Meteora, and is built on the left bank of the River Peneus on the southern outcrops of the rocks of Meteora at a height of 240 metres above sea level.

Near Kalambaka, according to the experts, was the ancient city of Aiginion, as confirmed by Strabo. He states that it was a city of the Tymphaeans and had common borders with Aithikia and Trikki, being built at the confluence of the rivers Ionas and Peneus. Following the famous battle of Pydna, Aiginion refused to submit to the Roman consul, Paulus Aemilius, and as a result was conquered and looted by the Romans

(Livy 32, 15). Votive columns, inscriptions and other architectural features which have come to light from time to time and which belong to that period have been built into the walls of the churches and other buildings of modern Kalambaka.

From the end of the tenth century modern Kalambaka was referred to by the name of Stagi and was the seat of a bishop. After 1204 Stagi was included in the domains of Michael Comnenos of Epirus. At the end of the 13th century it was the property of the dukes of New Patrai (Hypati), while in 1304 it was taken by the Frankish barons. In 1334 Stagi once again became subject to the Despot of Epirus, John II.

*Carved wooden door in the Church of the Dorm:
of the Virgin at Kalamb*

A little later it became part of the territory of the Byzantine Emperor Andronikos Palaeologos and around 1348 came under the rule of the great Krai of the Serbs Stephen Dusan. From 1356 the greater part of Thessaly was the property of Symeon Ouresis Palaeologos, who was the step-brother of Stephen Dusan, and Stagi was included under his rule.

The place has been known chiefly as Kalambaka from the time of Turkish rule, when it was for purposes of administration under the Pasha of Larissa. In the 18th century it acquired its own school, while it took an active part in the uprising of Thessaly in 1854. In the battle which followed between Greeks and Turks the latter lost over 500 men and valuable military equipment. During the course of the centuries there has been a notable and uninterrupted contact between Kalambaka and Meteora on a national, spiritual and artistic level.

Church of the Dormition of the Virgin

 famous monument of Byzantine art, the Church of the Dormition of the Virgin was built in the first half of the 12th century by the Emperor Manuel Comnenos (1143-1180), as can be concluded from imperial and Patriarchal documents which have been copied and which are preserved on the left side of the outer narthex of the church. Others maintain that the church is the work of the seventh century, on the evidence of the position of the ambo in the middle of the nave, while others ascribe the monument to the 11th century as a result of a comparison of the architecture of the church with that of others in Kastoria and Serres which belong to that period. Better founded seems to be the view that the church belongs to the first half of the 12th century, as would appear from the bull of the Patriarch Antony which is to be found written up

in the outer narthex of the church. The first two refer to murals and the last to a bell tower. The church is an aisled basilica, without dome, and with a roof sloping on both sides over the central aisle. The two roofs on the flanking aisles are lower. The length of the church, which is divided into outer narthex, narthex, main church and sanctuary, is 30 metres and it is 13 metres wide.

The Ambo

n the space in front of the central door of the screen and towards the middle of the central aisle stands a marble ambo made up of masonry from an early Christan ambo. Access to it is by a stair to the east and west of five steps each. With a right-angled centre, the ambo supports its upper section on four columns which stand on oblique marble beams, which are, in turn, supported by four small cylinders in the lower parts

Ambo. Reconstruction (A. Orlandos).

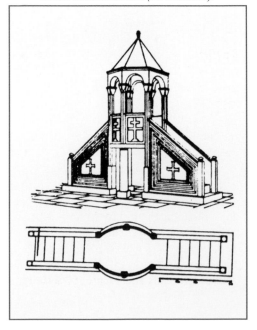

and on parapets with large carved crosses. The small marble cylinders have crosses in circles and the parapets are decorated with crosses and band designs. Various icon compositions, which certainly belong to a later period from 1669, may be seen above the parapets. On the western side there is the following inscription, which refers to the last repairs to the ambo:

THIS AMBO OF OUR LADY, MORE-THAN-HOLY MOTHER OF GOD AND EVER VIRGIN MARY, WAS DECORAT-ED BY THE AID AND AT THE EXPENSE OF THE BISHOP OF THE MOST HOLY SEE OF STAGI, MASTER DANIEL, MOST BELOVED OF GOD... IT WAS DECO-RATED BY THE HAND OF MASTER NICHOLAS IOANNIKIOS TOGETHER WITH HIS CHILDREN IN 1669

The Ciborium and Synthronon

f particular note in this church are the marble ciborium and the syn-thronon, which are in the sanctu-ary. The ciborium is believed to be older than the 11th century and is supported on four columns. The arches are decorated with three crosses in circles. The heads of the small columns are deco-rated with four vine leaves each, i.e. on each side. On the angles there are stylized grapes resembling a kind of pine cone. The syn-thronon is to the east of the altar. It consists of four semi-circular steps and the episco-pal throne where the celebrant sat when not preaching or officiating. Under the syn-thronon is a large crypt where the liturgical vessels of the church were kept and where the Christians hid in times of persecution.

The screen of the church belongs to the 17th century. It is gilded and instead of col-umning it has beams with double decoration above low reliefs and simple spiral designs.

Synthronon within the Sanctuary.

The Murals

The church is decorated with icon compositions which belong to the historical, doctrinal and liturgical cycle of the Orthodox Church. A few of the murals belong to the 13th or 14th centuries, while the rest are of the 16th, as is confirmed by an inscription above the door outside the narthex.

The sacristy of the church was on the east side of the Diaconicon. On the right of the entrance to the sacristy a sarcophagus built into the wall is to be found. Advice as to Christian behaviour is written up on the outside of the east wall, where there are also various carvings belonging to the Classical and Roman periods.

At a depth of 25 cms. below the present floor of the sanctuary, a section of mosaic flooring, measuring 1.80 x 5.65 metres and showing a peacock amid branches and pomegranates, was found recently.

Church of St. John the Baptist: This church is to be found near the market of Ka-lambaka and was built in 1336.

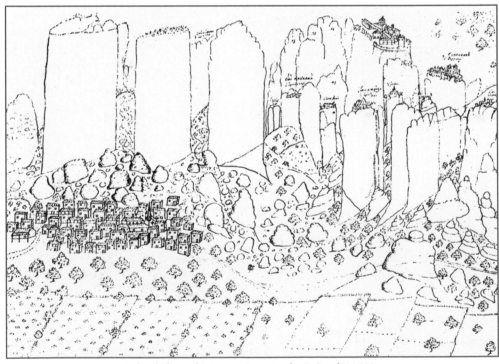

Kalambaka and Meteora. Drawing by B. Barskij 1745.

KASTRAKI

Two kilometres north west of Kalambaka, on the western foothills of the Meteora rocks and at a height of 270 metres above sealevel, stands Kastraki, an attractive village whose houses huddle together in an amphitheatre below the heavy mass of the Meteora rocks. Its first inhabitants, according to tradition, were Epirots who left the parts of Northern Epirus where they lived because they could not stand the atrocities of Ali Pasha and came to Kalambaka. From there they went to the north west and reached a point where there were the ruins of a castle and founded the hamlets of Rouxiori, Ayia Paraskevi, Rigilavo and Triskiano. A little later, that is, at the beginning of the 18th century, these hamlets were united to form the village of Kastraki. The name comes, without doubt, from the Byzantine castle ('kastro') which used to stand there, the ruins of which survive to this day. The Kastro was built by the Byzantine Emperor Andronikos Palaeologos and stood until 1362. It was here that the administrator of the district, known as the 'head', had his headquarters.

Today Kastraki has 1261 inhabitants and is proud of its history, firm in its traditions and sure of its beauty. The smiling and cheerful inhabitants are ready to provide for all visitors, and for each one individually, all the products which their area is rich in.

BIBLIOGRAPHY

ADAMANTIOU *A Proceedings of the Archaeological Society. Athens 1909.*

ARVANITOPOULOS A. *Thessalian Monuments. Athens 1909.*

BARSONKOY N. *Zimjitrudy B.C. Batkago (Life and Works of B.C. Barskij) St. Petersburg 1885.*

VEIS N. *Contribution to the History of the Monasteries of Meteora, 'Vizantis' Vol. A (1909), pp. 208 et seq. (1911) pp. 1 et seq.*
— *Byzantinisch Neugriectiische Jahrbiicher, Vol. C (1922), pp. 364 et seq.*
— *Manuscripts of Meteora (Academy of Athens publication), Athens 1967*
— *Christophoros Varlaamitis and his Short Chronicle, Epirot Chronicles Vol. A (1926) pp. 63 et seq.*

VOYIATZIDIS I. *Meteora, 'Athina' magazine Vol. 24 (1912), p.p. 346 et seq., Yearbook of the Society for Byzantine Studies, Vol. A (1924), pp. 139 et seq., Vol. B (1925), pp. 149 et seq.*

(VIKINIOS) *T. Kalambaka, «Panthessalian Album» A Volos (1927), p. 39. The Monasteries of Meteora, vide pp. 96-99, The Monastery of the Transfiguration, vide pp. 128-133. The Monastery of St. Stephen, vide pp. 228-234. The Monastery of the Holy Trinity, vide pp. 374-376.*

GEORGIADES N. *Thessaly, Volos 1894.*

GRAVANIS *Sophronios (Archimandrite) St. Nicholas Anapafsas. Athens.*

DIONYSIOS *Metropolitan of Trikki and Stragi, Meteora. Athens 1976.*

DOUSMANIS V. *History of Thessaly. Athens 1925.*

ZOSIMAS ESPHIGMENITIS *(Monk) Meteora. 'Phimi' journal. Volos 1878.*

THEOTEKNI *(Nun) The Stone Forest of Meteora. Athens 1975.*
— *The Martyrology of Meteora. Athens 1975.*
— *On the Rock of the Angelic City. Athens 1977.*
— *Meteora: History, Art, Monastic Life. Athens 1980.*

KALOKYRIS K. *Theophanis the Cretan. Encyclopaedia of Religion and Ethics, Vol. 5. Athens 1965.*
— *Origin of the Byantine Monuments in the Geographical Area of Macedonia, Serbia and Bulgaria. Thessaloniki 1970.*

KARAMANOS K. *'Kalambaka'Great Greek Encyclopaedia, Vol. 13, pp. 532 et seq.*

KOUROS A. *Meteora. Athens 1965.*

KOKKINIS S. *The Museums of Greece. Athens.*
— *The Monasteries of Greece. Athens.*

NIMAS T. *(Editor) Index to the periodical 'Meteora' (publication of the Touring and Cultural Club of Trikala). Trikala, 1978.*

ORLANDOS A. *Monastic Architecture. Athens, 1917.*

PAPADOPOULOS S. *Western Thessaly - Meteora. publ. Pechlivanidis, Athens.*

PAPASOTIRIOU I. *Meteora. Trikala 1964.*

PAPASTERGIOU C. *The tourist development of the Prefecture of Trikala. 'Proinos Logos' newspaper, Tues. 2 Oct. 1979.*

PISTAS I. *(Monastic Steward) The Church of the Dormition of the Virgin in Kalabaka. Athens 1977.*

PIOBINOS P. *Greek Icon Painters up to 1821. Athens 1979.*

PROVATAKIS T. *Meteora (illustrated guide) Athens 1978.*
— *Sixty Cretan Icon Painters of the Postbyzantine Period. Thessaloniki 1977. (Reprint).*

PROVATAKIS *Thomas. Orthodox Art and Tradition. Thessaloniki 1972.*

RAMMIDIS P. *(Abbot) Meteora. Athens 1882.*

SISILIANOS D. *Greek Icon Painters after the Fall of Constantinople. Athens 1935.*

SCOUVARAS V. *Archaeological and Tourist Guide to Thessaly. Volos 1958.*
— *Meteora. Volos 1951.*

SOTIRIOU G. *Byzantine Monuments of Thessaly of the 13th and 14th Centuries. Yearbook of the Society for Byzantine Studies, Vol. 11 (1932) Athens.*

STOURNARAS N. *Meteora. Athens.*

CHRYSOCHOIDIS C. *Designs from the Manuscript Work of Basil Grigorovich Barskij from the first photolithographical printing in the edition of 1885-1887.*

TOPOS KAI EIKONA.
— *Engravings of Foreign Travellers in Greece, 18th century. Publ. OLKOS. Athens 1979.*

STATISTICS

eteora is in the Prefecture of Trikkala, Thessaly, and stands at approximately 600 metres above sea level and 400 from the opening of the Peneus into the Thessalian plain. Distance in kilometres from: Kalambaka - 5, Trikkala - 26, Larissa - 88, Thessaloniki - 230, Volos 145, Athens - 331 and Ioannina - 110. The Prefecture of Trikkala has an area of 3,338 square kilometres and a population of 132,519. The capital is Trikkala.

DAYS AND TIMES AT WHICH THE METEORA MONASTERIES MAY BE VISITED

	WINTER	SUMMER
GREAT METEORO MONASTERY (OF THE TRANSFORMATION)	9.00-16.00 Tues, Weds closed	9.00-17.00 Tuesday closed
VARLAAM MONASTERY	9.00-15.00 Thurs, Friday closed	9.00-16.00 Friday closed
ST. STEPHEN'S NUNNERY	9.00-13.30 & 15.30-17.30 Monday closed	9.00-13.30 & 15.30-17.30 Monday closed
HOLY TRINITY TRINITY MONASTERY	9.00-14.00 Tues, Thursday closed	9.00-17.00 Thursday closed
MONASTERY OF ST. NICHOLAS THE RELIEVER	9.00-16.00 Tues, Weds closed	9.00-17.00 Tuesday closed
ROUSANOU MONASTERY	9.00-14.00 Wednesday closed	9.00-18.00 Wednesday closed

TELEPHONE NUMBERS OF THE METEORA MONASTERIES

GREAT METEORO MONASTERY (OF THE TRANSFORMATION)....... 2432-022278

VARLAAM MONASTERY.. 2432-022277

ST. STEPHEN'S NUNNERY 2432-022279

HOLY TRINITY TRINITY MONASTERY....................................... 2432-022220

MONASTERY OF ST. NICHOLAS THE RELIEVER 2432-022375

ROUSANOU MONASTERY 2432-022649

SHOPPING

There is an ample variety of popular products in the market of Kalabaka, as well as in the whole region. You can find multi-colored textiles (dyed in natural paints), hand-made carpets (well-known as 'flokati') and various wooden house tools. Icons painted in the Byzantine style by monks who live in the monasteries on the Meteora rocks, have in their back a seal of an eagle with the two heads, a sign of a genuine creation and for a free exportation. There is also a great number of chains, crosses, calendars, plates and other folk art items.

Text by: THEOCHARIS M. PROVA TAKIS
Art Work: B7. BARSKU, A. ORLANDOS, F. KONTOGLOU, R. KOPSIDES

Photography by permition of the Bischopric of Trikki and Stagon (Permit Nr. 507/17-5-1980).